OVID IN LOVE

OVID IN LOVE

Ovid's *Amores*
translated by
GUY LEE
and with drawings by
JOHN WARD

Thomas Dunne Books
St. Martin's Press
New York

Typeset in 9.25/11pt Palatino by Wearset, Boldon, Tyne & Wear
Printed and bound by G Canale, Torino, Italy

CONTENTS

BOOK ONE

BOOK TWO

BOOK THREE

BOOK ONE

Farewell to Epic

My epic was under construction – wars and armed violence
in the grand manner, with metre matching theme.

I had written the second hexameter when Cupid grinned
and calmly removed one of its feet.

'You young savage' I protested 'poetry's none of your business.
We poets are committed to the Muses.

Imagine Venus grabbing Minerva's armour
and Minerva brandishing love's torch!

Imagine Ceres queen of the mountain forests
and Diana the huntress running a farm!

Or long-haired Phoebus doing pike drill
and Mars strumming the seven-stringed lyre!

You've a large empire, my boy – too much power already.
Why so eager for extra work?

Or is the whole world yours – the glens of Helicon included?
Can't Phoebus call his lyre his own these days?

Page one line one of my epic rises to noble heights
but line two lowers the tone

and I haven't the right subject for light verse –
a pretty boy or girl with swept-up hair.'

In reply the god undid his quiver and pulled out
an arrow with my name on it.

'Poet' he said, flexing the bow against his knee,
'I'll give you something to sing about – take that!'

Alas his arrows never miss. My blood's on fire.
Love has moved in as master of my heart.

I choose the couplet – rising six feet, falling five.
Farewell, hexameters and iron wars.

Garland your golden hair with myrtle from the seaside,
hendecametric Muse, my Elegia.

Insomnia

What's wrong with me I wonder? This mattress feels so hard.
The blankets won't stay on the bed.

I haven't slept a wink – tossing and turning
all night long. And now I'm aching all over.

Can it be love? Surely I'd know if it were?
Or does love work under cover and strike unobserved?

Yes, those phantom arrows must have pierced my heart
and relentless Cupid is torturing me.

Shall I give in? Or fan the flame by fighting it?
Better give in. Balance makes a burden light.

Shake a torch and it flares up –
leave it alone and it dies.

A bullock restive under the yoke
gets beaten more than his patient partner.

Spirited horses bruise their mouths on the bit;
the docile seldom feel it.

The god of love hits rebels far harder
than his submissive slaves.

Then I submit, Cupid. I'm your latest victim
standing here with my hands up.

The war's over. I'm suing for peace and pardon.
There's no glory in shooting an unarmed man.

Bind your hair with myrtle. Harness your mother's doves.
Vulcan will fit you out with a chariot.

Mount it and steer your doves through the crowd
as they hail you victor.

You too can celebrate a glorious Triumph
with young men and girls as your prisoners of war

and I'll be among them wearing my new chains
nursing this open wound – your abject slave.

Conscience and Common Sense and all Love's enemies
will be dragged along with hands tied behind their backs.

You'll strike fear into all hearts.
The crowd will worship you, chanting *Io Triumphe*.

12

Your loyal irregulars Flattery, Passion and Illusion
will act as bodyguard,

the forces that bring you victory over gods and men,
providing cover for your nakedness.

Your laughing mother will watch the Triumph from Olympus
and clap her hands and shower you with roses

as you ride along, jewels flashing from wings and hair,
a golden boy in a golden chariot,

raising many a fire if I know you,
wounding many a heart as you pass by,

your arrows willy-nilly never resting,
the flame of your torch scorching at close range,

a god mighty as Bacchus along the Ganges,
your doves terrible as tigers.

Then spare me for your Triumph.
Don't waste your strength on me

but imitate your conquering cousin Augustus –
he turns his conquests into protectorates.

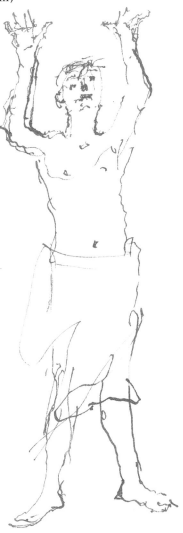

The Proposal

Thief of my heart, it's only fair
you should give me yours or cherish mine for ever.

No, I'm asking too much – simply let me love you
and Venus will have answered all my prayers.

I'll be your slave for life,
your ever faithful lover.

I can't claim noble ancestry,
my father's a mere knight,

my acres are hardly broad,
my allowance barely enough.

But Phoebus and the Nine are with me,
the wine-god and the god of love,

fidelity, integrity,
sincerity, sensitivity.

I'm no philanderer leaping from bed to bed.
I promise to be yours for ever.

O for the luck to live with you while life's thread lasts,
and to die while you weep beside me!

You shall be theme and inspiration,
my verse the mirror of your merit.

Io the timid heifer,
Leda who loved a swan,

Europa at sea, holding tight to a bull's horns,
these owe fame to verse.

Verse can make *us* world-famous too,
linking our names – together always.

The Dinner Party

Your husband? Going to the same dinner as us?
I hope it chokes him.

So I'm only to gaze at you, darling? Play gooseberry,
while another man enjoys your touch?

You'll lie there snuggling up to him? He'll put his arm
round your neck whenever he wants?

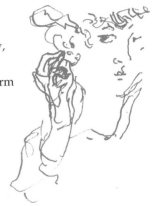

No wonder Centaurs fought over Hippodamia
when the wedding wine began to flow.

I don't live in the forest nor am I part horse
but I find it hard to keep my hands off you.

However here's my plan. Listen carefully.
Don't throw my words of wisdom to the winds.

Arrive before him – not that I see what good
arriving first will do but arrive first all the same.

When he takes his place on the couch and you go to join him
looking angelic, secretly touch my foot.

Watch me for nods and looks that talk
and unobserved return my signals

in the language of eyebrows and fingers
with annotations in wine.

Whenever you think of our love-making
stroke that rosy cheek with your thumb.

If you're cross with me, darling,
press the lobe of your ear

but turn your ring round if you're pleased
with anything I say or do.

When you feel like cursing your fool of a husband
touch the table as if you were praying.

If he mixes you a drink, beware – tell him to drink it himself,
then quietly ask the waiter for what you want.

I'll intercept the glass as you hand it back
and drink from the side you drank from.

Refuse all food he has tasted first –
it has touched his lips.

Don't lean your gentle head against his shoulder
and don't let him embrace you

or slide a hand inside your dress
or touch your breasts. Above all don't kiss him.

If you do I'll cause a public scandal,
grab you and claim possession.

I'm bound to see all this. It's what I shan't see
that worries me – the goings on under your cloak.

Don't press your thigh or leg against his
or touch his coarse feet with your toes.

I know all the tricks. That's why I'm worried.
I hate to think of him doing what I've done.

We've often made love under your cloak, sweetheart,
in a glorious race against time.

You won't do that, I know. Still,
to avoid all doubt don't wear one.

Encourage him to drink but mind – no kisses.
Keep filling his glass when he's not looking.

If the wine's too much for him and he drops off
we can take our cue from what's going on around us.

When you get up to leave and we all follow
move to the middle of the crowd.

You'll find me there – or I'll find you
so touch me anywhere you can.

But what's the good? I'm only temporizing.
Tonight decrees our separation.

Tonight he'll lock you in and leave me
desolated at your door.

Then he'll kiss you, then go further,
forcing his right to our secret joy.

But you *can* show him you're acting under duress.
Be mean with your love – give grudgingly – in silence.

He won't enjoy it if my prayers are answered.
And if they're not, at least assure me you won't.

But whatever happens tonight tell me tomorrow
you didn't sleep with him – and stick to that story.

17

The Siesta

Siesta time in sultry summer.
I lay relaxed on the divan.

One shutter closed, the other ajar,
made sylvan semi-darkness,

a glimmering dusk, as after sunset,
or between night's end and day's beginning –

the half light shy girls need
to hide their hesitation.

At last – Corinna. On the loose in a short dress,
long hair parted and tumbling past the pale neck –

lovely as Lais of the many lovers,
Queen Semiramis gliding in.

I grabbed the dress; it didn't hide much,
but she fought to keep it,

only half-heartedly though.
Victory was easy, a self-betrayal.

There she stood, faultless beauty
in front of me, naked.

Shoulders and arms challenging eyes and fingers.
Nipples firmly demanding attention.

Breasts in high relief above the smooth belly.
Long and slender waist. Thighs of a girl.

Why list perfection?
I hugged her tight.

The rest can be imagined – we fell asleep.
Such afternoons are rare.

Locked Out

Porter! – poor wretch, chained like a dog –
please open up.

I don't ask much – a mere crack
so there's room to squeeze through sideways.

Love has made me slim enough,
halved my weight and alerted my limbs.

He can teach you to slip past sentries –
never lets you put a foot wrong.

I used to be scared of the dark –
admired people who went out at night.

But Cupid and his mother, laughing in my ear,
whispered 'You too can be brave'

and brought me love. I'm not afraid of ghosts now
or hands raised to strike me down.

It's only you I'm frightened of. You're so slow.
It's only you who make me crawl. Your bolt can destroy me.

Just look at this door. Unbar it so you can see.
It's all wet with my tears.

That day you were stripped for a whipping – remember? –
I got your mistress to let you off.

I helped you then and now you won't help me.
Do you call that fair?

One good turn deserves another. Now's your chance to thank me.
The night is slipping by. Unbar the door.

And soon you'll be rid of your long chain,
drinking the wine of freedom at last . . .

Porter, you're hard. You can hear me pleading
but this heavy door hasn't moved an inch.

Beleaguered cities bar their gates.
But why be afraid of weapons in peacetime?

Lock out lovers and what have you left for enemies?
The night is slipping by. Unbar the door.

I'm not here with an armed guard –
I'd be alone if cruel Love weren't with me.

I could never dismiss *him* –
I'd have to be dismembered first.

So there's me, and Love, and a little wine (gone to my head),
and a garland askew on my damp hair.

Who's afraid of an outfit like that? Who wouldn't welcome it?
The night is slipping by. Unbar the door.

Perhaps you're asleep, damn you,
and my words aren't sinking in.

But you stayed awake till starry midnight
in the old days when I tried to slip out.

Or have you a girl-friend in your cell?
If so you're better off than me.

To be with mine I'd gladly wear your chain.
The night is slipping by. Unbar the door.

Listen! Did those hinges creak?
Was that something hitting the door? . . .

Only a gust of wind against it
blowing my poor hopes out of reach.

Ah Boreas, if you still remember the bride you ravished
blow this way and bang on these deaf panels . . .

Silence in Rome, and bright dew falling,
and *night slipping by. Unbar the door.*

Or I'll use my torch's fire and steel
to teach this lordly house a lesson.

Night and wine and love can't abide half measures.
Love and wine are fearless. Night has no shame . . .

I've tried everything. Threats and entreaties are useless.
This oak has a softer heart than yours.

Guarding the door of a pretty girl?
You ought to be a prison warder.

And now the morning star looms in a frosty sky.
Cocks are crowing to wake the world's workers.

I'm out of luck. I'll pull this garland off my head
and throw it down on the doorstep.

My love will see it lying there
in token of a wasted night.

Meanwhile, you oafish locker-out of lovers,
I do you the honour of saying goodbye.

You too, stone steps, deaf posts, and wooden door,
goodbye – and thanks for your servility.

The Quarrel

Tie up my hands, any friend of mine here,
tie them up till I'm sane again – they deserve it.

In a fit of madness I hit my love,
hurt her and made her cry.

In that state I could have hit my own mother
or taken a whip to the holy gods.

I was mad as Homeric Ajax
when he massacred the flocks,

mad as Orestes the matricide
when he threatened to fight the Furies.

How could I do it? How could I ravel that perfect hair?
Yet ravelled hair became her –

she still looked lovely, like Atalanta
shooting beasts in Arcadia,

or Ariadne in tears while the south wind
blew Theseus and his promises away,

or Cassandra kneeling at Athena's altar,
except that *she* was wearing a headband.

'Crazy brute!' I can hear you saying
but she said nothing – she was too afraid.

Her eyes were my accusation though
and I read my sentence in her tears.

I'd sooner my arms had dropped from their sockets –
I'd have done better without them.

Victim of my own violence
I used a madman's strength to punish myself.

These hands are instruments of crime and bloodshed –
guilty of sacrilege. Chain them up.

If I struck the humblest citizen I'd pay for it:
have I any more right to strike my mistress?

Diomede set an evil precedent:
he was the first man to wound a goddess – and I'm the second.

But he had more excuse. He was fighting an enemy.
I hurt the girl I professed to love.

Come on. conquering hero, get ready for your Triumph.
Wear your laurels and give God the glory.

There'll be a fine procession all shouting
'Hurrah for the hero who beat his girl!'

She'll walk in front, a poor prisoner, with ravelled hair,
pale as a ghost, except for the bruises on her cheeks.

I'd rather her neck were marked
black and blue with love-bites.

If I had to give way to a flood of rage,
to blind fury,

couldn't I merely have shouted and stormed
to frighten her – not too much?

Or ripped her dress down to the waist
where the belt would have saved it?

But no. I behaved like a brute,
grabbing her hair, scratching her cheeks.

She stood there dazed. Her face
went white as Parian marble.

Her body froze, But I could see her trembling
like aspen leaves in a breath of air

or slender reeds when the breeze blows softly
or water ruffled by a summer wind.

Her tears welled up, hung there, and at last brimmed over
like snow melting.

It was then I knew what I had done –
those tears were my life-blood.

Three times I tried to clasp her feet and beg forgiveness,
three times she pushed my hands away – terrified.

Don't wait, my dear. Revenge is sweet.
Dig your nails in my face – now.

Show my hair and my eyes no mercy.
Anger will give you strength.

Or at least remove the grim evidence of my crime
and discipline that wild hair again.

The Madam

There's someone I know – if you want to meet a Madam read on –
there's an old bitch I know called Dipsas.

What better name for her? Rosy Dawn
has never seen her sober.

She's the local witch –
can reverse the flow of water,

whirl the magic wheel, cull herbs,
brew aphrodisiacs,

guarantee the weather,
cloud or sunshine,

blood-red stars (believe it or not)
or a bloody moon – I've seen both.

She's a night-bird – probably flits about
in owlish feathers.

That's what people say. And her eyes
are twin-pupilled, glinting double.

She's necromantic too
and chants earth-splitting spells.

Well, this creature tried to corrupt my innocent girl
and she's very persuasive – poisonously so.

The door was open. I happened to overhear
the following lecture:

'You know, my dear, you made quite a hit yesterday
with that rich young man. He couldn't take his eyes off you.

And no wonder. You're beautiful – no one more so.
It's such a pity you don't make the most of yourself.

I want that lovely face to be your fortune –
I know you'd never let old Dipsas starve.

With Mars in opposition the luck was against you
but Venus in Libra has turned the golden scale

and look how your luck has changed! Here's a rich lover
pining to satisfy your every need!

He's handsome too – almost as pretty as you are.
If he weren't so keen to buy *you* we'd have to buy *him*.

She's blushing! – Yes, modesty suits a pale skin
but it's better put on – the real thing can be a nuisance.

You must look demurely down at your lap and ration your glances
to suit the value of each lover's gift.

I know those Sabine frumps refused to be obliging
but that was in King Tatius' bad old days.

Today Mars is kept so busy fighting abroad
that Venus has things all her own way in Rome.

Pretty girls play. Chaste means never asked.
If you're really smart you do your own asking.

Those girls that hold up their hands in horror –
look at them closer – they're praying for a lover.

Even Penelope sized up her suitors –
got them to draw that bow of horn.

Time slips past. We don't notice it passing
but the years slip by at a gallop.

It's use that makes bronze shine. Pretty dresses need wearing.
Neglected property falls to rack and ruin.

Your beauty needs exercise. It will soon fade
if you don't take lovers – and one or two aren't enough.

Best have a crowd to fleece, like the grey wolf.
It's a surer way and much less obvious.

Now take this poet of yours – he sends you his collections
but you'd collect far more from a proper lover.

Poets ought to be rich. Apollo their patron god
wears cloth of gold and twangs a golden lyre.

Homer's great but the man who can give is greater.
Giving's a fine art, you know.

Never look down on an ex-slave with money.
What if his feet *were* coated with chalk?

And don't be fooled by family portraits. If a lover's broke
out he goes – and great-great-grandad with him.

Don't give a boy a free night because he's handsome –
tell him to raise the cash from one of his men-friends first.

Easy does it while you're setting the trap
but once he's caught squeeze him – hard as you like.

It does no harm to pretend you love him
provided you sell him the idea.

Don't always say yes: say you've a headache –
say you must go and worship Isis.

But don't overdo it. He may get used to feeling low
and his love cool off if you disappoint him too often.

Slam your door on serenades. Open it wide to presents.
Let lucky A hear B in the porch protesting.

You've wronged him? *You* are the injured party. Lose your temper.
Counter his grievance – he'll soon forget it.

But never be angry for long –
that only makes enemies.

And another thing: you must practise crying.
Specialise in tears of jealousy.

When you're deceiving him don't be afraid to swear you're not.
Venus never listens to lovers' lies.

You'll need a clever maid and a manservant to help
by telling him what gifts to get you.

They can ask for tips as well –
many a mickle makes a muckle.

Your mother and sister can cash in too – and your old nanny.
Many hands, quick money.

If you're short of excuses for presents
wheel in the birthday cake.

Never let him take you for granted. Give him a rival.
Love thrives on competition.

Let him notice signs of another man in the bed
and a bruise or two on your neck.

Above all show him X's presents. If there aren't any
order them on appro – from the Via Sacra.

When he's given a lot vary your tactics and ask for a loan
which of course you'll never repay.

Be devious and chat him up. Sting as you kiss.
Honey hides the taste of poison.

In all my long experience I've never known these tips to fail.
So take my advice and don't be a scatter-brain.

Many's the time you'll bless me while I'm still alive
and pray my bones lie easy when I'm gone . . .'

Her voice droned on but my shadow gave me away.
I was itching to get my hands

on that wispy white hair, those baggy cheeks
and bleary alcoholic eyes.

God give her nowhere to live, a penniless old age,
chronic winters, and an insatiable thirst!

Love's Military Service

Yes, Atticus, take it from me –
lovers are all soldiers, in Cupid's private army.

Military age equals amatory age –
fighting and making love don't suit the old.

Commanders expect gallantry of their men –
and so do pretty girls.

Lovers too keep watch, bivouac, mount guard –
at their mistress' door instead of H.Q.

They have their forced marches,
tramping miles for love,

crossing rivers, climbing mountains,
trudging through the snow.

Ordered abroad they brave the storm
and steer by winter stars.

Hardened to freezing nights,
to showers of hail and sleet,

they go out on patrol,
observe their rival's movements,

lay siege to rebel mistresses
and batter down front doors.

Tacticians recommend the night attack,
use of the spearhead, catching the foe asleep.

These tactics wiped out Rhesus and his Thracians,
capturing the famous horses.

Lovers use them too – to exploit a sleeping husband,
thrusting hard while the enemy snores,

eluding guards and night patrols,
moving under cover.

If war's a gamble, love's a lottery. Both have ups and downs.
In both apparent heroes can collapse.

So think again if you think of love as a soft option –
it calls for enterprise and courage.

Achilles loved Briseis, sulked when he lost her –
Trojans, now's your chance to hammer the Greeks!

Andromache strapped Hector's helmet on
and sent him into battle with a kiss.

Great Agamemnon fell in love at first sight –
with Cassandra's wind-swept hair.

Even Mars was caught. Trapped in the blacksmith's net
he caused an epic scandal in the sky.

And what about me? I was soft – born in a dressing-gown.
A reading-couch in the shade had sapped my morale.

But a pretty girl soon put me on my feet –
Fall in she ordered, *follow me.*

And look at me now – alive and alert, the night-fighter.
Yes, if you want an active life try love.

Love and Presents

You were my Helen, Ilion-bound from Sparta
to cause a war between two husbands,

my Leda, seduced by the white feathers
of a lecherous god,

my Amymone, lost in arid Argos,
balancing a pitcher on coiled hair,

and for your sake I was afraid of the eagle and the bull,
afraid of all Jove's amorous disguises.

But now, those fears are gone, my delusion cured.
Your face no longer haunts me.

Why am I changed? You keep asking for presents.
That's why I find you unattractive.

While you were straight with me I loved you body and soul,
but this inner twist disfigures the outer you.

Love is a naked child. His tender years
and the missing clothes are symbols of innocence.

Why ask the son of Venus to sell himself?
He wears no money-belt.

He and his mother hate aggression,
deserve better than mercenaries' pay.

Even a prostitute, earning a bare living,
everybody's at a price, compliant,

curses the ponce she is forced to obey.
You are different – you can choose.

Learn from the animals – they don't calculate.
Brutes have kinder hearts than yours.

Do mares ask stallions for presents? Do cows ask bulls?
Do rams need presents to court their favourite ewes?

It's only women who love to plunder their lovers,
who hire out their nights and auction their bodies,

who sell shares in desire and joy
at a price that suits their selfish pleasure.

When love brings equal happiness to two people
why should either buy it from the other?

Why should sex, a co-operative venture,
be credited to your account and debited to mine?

If it's wrong for witnesses to be suborned,
for judges on the panel to accept bribes,

for defending counsel to be paid money,
for a court's proceedings to end in proceeds,

it's equally wrong to capitalize free love
and cash in on beauty.

Services rendered gratis rightly earn gratitude;
hired intercourse earns none.

Payment frees the customer from all commitment –
he owes you nothing for being obliging.

Beauty, beware. Think twice before taxing sex.
Greed can have nasty repercussions.

Settling for Sabine armlets Tarpeia
was crushed to death under Sabine arms.

In revenge for the bribe of a necklace
Alcmaeon murdered his own mother.

However, it's not improper to ask the rich for presents –
they can well afford them.

Pick your grapes from prolific vines
and raid Alcinous' orchards

but let the poor man pay in kindness, loyalty, and love.
He can give his mistress all he has.

My special gift is verse, the praise of true beauty.
If I choose, my art can make you famous.

Dresses tear, jewels and golden trinkets break,
but poetic fame is a lasting present.

I'm ready to give but I hate your vulgar demands for payment.
Cut out demand and I'll supply.

The Go-between

Napë, the coiffeuse,
no ordinary maid,

backstage-manager of my love-life,
my silent prompter,

keeper of Corinna's conscience,
averting crisis –

please, Napë, take her this note,
immediately.

You're flesh and blood,
no fool.

You must have suffered in Cupid's wars
so help a comrade in arms.

If she asks about me, say I live for our next meeting.
This note will explain.

But I'm wasting time. Hand it to her when she's free,
make sure she reads it then and there,

and watch her face meanwhile –
there's prophecy in faces.

See she replies at once – a long letter.
Blank wax is a bore.

Get her to space the lines close and fill the margins
so it takes me longer to read.

Wait. Why tire her fingers pushing a stylus?
YES will do, in huge block capitals.

I'll garland those writing-tablets with Victory's laurel
and hang them up in the temple of Venus

above this dedication:
'From Naso – in wooden gratitude.'

The Flyting

Weep for my failure – writing-tablets returned
with a sorry answer: *Can't manage today.*

The superstitious are right. Napë stubbed her toe
on the step as she left.

You must have been drinking, my girl.
Next time be more careful, and pick your feet up.

Damn these obstructive lumps of wood,
this wax frustration

obviously extracted
from Corsican hemlock honey,

coloured with cinnabar, I'm told,
but in fact – bloody.

The gutter's the place for this lumber
to be crunched under passing wheels.

I'm sure the man who made them
had felon's hands.

The tree they came from hanged a suicide –
supplied the executioner with crosses.

Horned owls hooted in its branches,
vultures and screech-owls brooded there.

I was mad to entrust these
with tender messages.

They were meant for deadly legal instruments
in the hands of some commissioner for oaths,

or to be wedged among a usurer's ledgers,
recording his bad debts.

Double-tablets? Double-crossers!
They say two's an unlucky number.

God rot their wood with worm
and their wax with white mildew!

Aubade

Here she comes, over the sea from her poor old husband,
frosty axle turning, bringing the yellow day.

Why hurry, Aurora? Hold your horses, for Memnon's sake
and the annual sacrifice of his birds.

Now's the time when I love to lie in my love's soft arms,
the time of times to feel her body close to mine,

the time when sleep is heavy, the air cold,
and birdsong sweetest.

Why hurry? Lovers hate your company.
Tighten the reins in your rosy fingers.

Before your coming sailors can better watch their stars
and keep their course in open waters.

Travellers however tired rise when you appear
and soldiers reach for their weapons.

Your eye first lights on peasants shouldering their mattocks
and drags oxen under the yoke.

You rob children of sleep, condemn them
to classrooms and the cruel cane.

You send the unwary down to the Forum
to give their one-word promise and lose thousands.

Learned counsel deprecate your summons
to rise and shine again in court.

Back to the distaff and the daily stint
you call the housewife when her hands could idle.

I could stand all this, but pretty girls rising at dawn –
no lover can endure it.

If only night would defy you,
and the stars stare you out!

If only the wind would break your axle,
or frozen cloud give your team a fall!

Why hurry, spoil-sport? – Does Memnon's black skin
reflect the colour of his mother's heart?

I wish Tithonus could gossip about you –
he'd kill your heavenly reputation.

You run away from him because he's old –
he hates you getting up so early.

But if you slept with Cephalus, you'd shout
'Oh gallop slow, you midnight horses!'

I know your husband's senile, but why should my love suffer?
Did I arrange your marriage?

The Moon let her Endymion sleep for years –
and she's quite as beautiful as you are.

Even Jupiter couldn't stand the sight of you
that time he joined two nights of love together. –

My final thrust. She must have heard me – she turned pink.
But the sun came up on time – as usual.

Disastrous Hair-dye

I told you to stop using that rinse,
and now you've no hair left to tint.

Why couldn't you let it be? It grew in such profusion,
falling below your hips,

so fine one felt setting would spoil it –
like strands of Chinese silk

or the gossamer a spider spins
hanging from a high rafter.

It wasn't dark and it wasn't golden –
it was both and neither,

like the underbark of a tall cedar
in a green valley on Mount Ida.

Obedient too, easy to style and set,
it never made you lose your temper.

Grips and side-combs didn't break it.
Your maid could feel safe –

I've often watched her setting it
and you never jabbed a pin in her arm.

And I've often seen you before the morning ritual
lying back on your lilac couch

with ravelled hair – a Maenad tired of the dancing,
relaxed on a Thracian lawn. It suited you like that.

But delicate, and soft as down
what tortures it had to endure,

braving rack and ordeal by fire
to be twisted in tight spirals!

'It's a crime' I cried 'a downright crime to singe that hair.
It suits you as it is. Unsteel your heart.

No violence, please. It's not for burning.
It can teach the tongs a trick or two.'

And now it's ruined – lovely hair
Apollo or Bacchus might have envied,

sleek as Dione's in the picture
where she rises naked from the waves.

You called it a mess and now you miss it. Silly girl,
don't put the mirror down so mournfully.

You must look at yourself with new eyes –
forget yourself if you want to be attractive.

It's not as if some rival had poisoned you
or a witch had washed you in unholy water.

You haven't been ill – touch wood –
and it wasn't the evil eye that thinned it.

You've only yourself to blame. You were asking for trouble
applying that concoction.

But thanks to our German triumph you're quite safe.
One of the women prisoners can send you hers.

The only trouble is when people admire it
you'll think 'I have to buy admiration now.

These compliments really belong to some Sygambrian girl.
Gone are the days when I deserved them.'

Poor dear, she's trying so hard not to cry,
shielding her face to hide the blushes,

staring down at the lost hair in her lap –
a keepsake regrettably misplaced.

Now put on your make-up and make up your mind the loss isn't final.
You'll soon be admired again – for home-grown hair.

Poetry Immortal

Devouring Envy, why accuse *me* of wasting my life?
Why call poetry idlers' work?

The young shirker! What? Not following tradition?
Not earning a soldier's dusty decorations?

Not memorizing tedious laws or touting
rhetoric in the fickle Forum?

But your work dies. I want undying fame –
alive and singing, always, everywhere.

Homer's alive while Tenedos and Ida stand
and Simois runs to the sea.

Hesiod's alive while grapes fill with juice
and wheat falls to the sickle.

Callimachus the unoriginal master
will sing on – everywhere and always.

Can Sophocles come to a tragic end?
Aratus is safe as sun and moon.

While servants cheat and fathers storm,
while ponces grab and tarts flatter, Menander survives.

Blunt Ennius – impassioned Accius –
are names time cannot touch.

Shall Varro be forgotten? Argo on the slipway?
Jason's quest for gold?

Sublime Lucretius will endure
till the day when all the world dissolves.

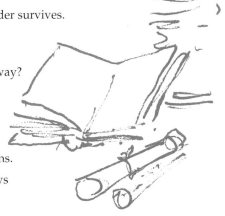

Arms and the man, Farming and *Tityrus*
will be read while Rome is above the nations.

While Cupid's armed with torch and arrows
men will prize Tibullan grace.

Western lands and the lands of sunrise
will remember Gallus – and his Lycoris.

Time can destroy flints, and iron ploughshares,
but poetry is indestructible,

greater than kings and their triumphs,
rarer than Spanish gold.

The crowd go for tinsel. I choose golden Apollo,
a cup brim-full of Castalian water,

a garland of sun-loving myrtle,
and my tormented audience – the lovers.

Envy feeds on the living but sleeps on tombs,
for each gets his due in the end.

Therefore beyond the last devouring flame
I too shall live – in the body of my work.

BOOK TWO

The Magic of Poetry

Another collection of verse by the man from Sulmona,
that embarrassingly personal poet Naso.

Another of Cupid's commissions. Hands off, moralists!
Love's tender strains will shock you.

I write for the girl who responds to her sweetheart,
and the boy in love for the first time.

I want every young man wounded like me by Cupid's bow
to recognize the symptoms of his fever

and ask himself in amazement 'How does this poet know
about me and my personal problems?'

Once, rashly, I sang of war in heaven and giants
with a hundred arms. My diction soared to the occasion –

the cruel vengeance of Mother Earth, and the piling
of Pelion upon Ossa upon Olympus.

But while I was busy with Jupiter standing on a storm-cloud,
thunderbolt at the ready to defend his heaven,

Corinna slammed her door. I dropped the thunderbolt
and even forgot the Almighty.

Forgive me, Lord. Your weapons couldn't help me.
That locked door had a far more effective bolt.

I returned to couplets and compliments, my own weapons,
and broke down its resistance with soft words.

The magic of verse can pull the blood-red moon out of orbit,
turn back the journeying sun's white steeds,

make rivers flow upstream,
split hooded snakes,

fling doors wide open, sliding
the strongest bolts from their staples.

What good are epic heroes to me – the two Atridae,
Achilles fleet of foot,

Ulysses wasting twenty years in war and wanderings,
Hector dragged in the dust by Greek horses?

But sing the praises of a lovely girl
and she'll pay for the song in person.

A fair reward. Those famous names are out –
their gratitude means nothing to me.

My poems are written at Cupid's dictation
to catch the eye of Beauty.

The Chaperone

Can you spare me a moment, Bagoas? You chaperone this lady
and I'd like a few tactful words with you.

I saw her yesterday – strolling in the colonnade
among the statues of the Danaids.

She took my fancy. I wrote at once to ask for a meeting
and back came the timid answer *It's not allowed.*

On asking why, I learnt that you were the trouble –
you take your duties too seriously.

Be sensible about them and stop making enemies –
when we're afraid of someone we wish him dead.

Her husband's equally foolish. Why bother to guard
what loses nothing if unprotected?

Well, let him cultivate his amorous illusions
and think that what has many admirers can be chaste.

But present *her* with a gift – freedom to have affairs,
and she'll repay you with *your* freedom.

As confidant you'd have her in your power.
You think that's risky? Well then, turn a blind eye.

If she's reading a note, assume it's from her mother.
If a stranger turns up, let him get to know you.

If she wants to visit a girl-friend supposed to be ill,
accept the invalid story and let her go.

If she keeps you waiting, don't get impatient –
just relax, chin on chest, and snore.

And don't ask what goes on at the temple of Isis
or fear the worst in the crooked Theatre. –

But a confidant can always count on tips –
and is there an easier job than saying nothing?

He can do no wrong – upset the happy home and not get beaten.
He's the king-pin – the other servants mere dirt.

Your mistress can spin the yarns and hide the facts.
What satisfies her, will satisfy the master too.

Though husband frowns and scowls, in the last resort
he'll do as his little wife says.

But now and then she must make a point of scolding *you*.
When she calls you a callous brute and pretends to cry

you can tax her with something easily explained away,
so you won't be believed even when telling the truth. ·

Take my advice and you'll win respect – your savings will mount
and very soon you'll be buying your freedom.

Informers end up with chains round their necks –
you must have seen them. Traitors languish in jail.

Remember Tantalus in his pool, dying for a drink, clutching
at fruit just out of reach – because he couldn't keep his mouth shut;

and Argus, Io's over-conscientious guard,
who died suddenly – but she became a goddess.

I've seen a man with his legs festering in shackles
because he forced a husband to know the truth.

He deserved worse, for his malice did double damage –
broke a man's heart and ruined a woman's reputation.

In fact no husband likes to hear tales about his wife.
They help no one, even if he listens.

If he's not in love, your evidence is wasted on him;
if he is, your sense of duty only makes him wretched.

Besides, unfaithfulness, even when blatant, is hard to prove.
The judge is prejudiced in his wife's favour.

If he's actually seen it, he'll still believe her flat denial,
condemn his own eyes and hoodwink himself.

She has only to burst into tears and he'll start sobbing too
and threatening to punish the tell-tale.

Why fight against odds? You're bound to be beaten, in both senses.
The accused is sitting pretty in her judge's lap.

We're not planning murder or coming together to brew poison.
I'm not flashing a drawn sword in front of you.

We're only asking your permission to make love.
Could any request be more considerate?

Poor you! Neither male nor female, unable to share
the joys of sex, and yet keeping a mistress!

The man who first castrated boys
should have suffered the wound he inflicted.

I know you'd be sympathetic and obliging
if you'd ever felt the warmth of love.

But you weren't meant to ride or handle weapons;
you'd look unnatural gripping a spear.

Leave that to men. Renounce male ambition
and act as aide-de-camp to your mistress.

Serve her well and she'll reward you.
Where would you be without her?

She's in her prime, ripe for enjoyment;
such loveliness shouldn't be wasted.

For all your restrictions, she could have deceived you;
where there's a will there's a way.

But it seemed more tactful to try persuasion first
and give you the chance to make a good investment.

The Confession

I daren't excuse my weak character
by arguing falsely in self-defence.

I confess. They say confession helps.
Why not be reckless – conduct my own prosecution?

I hate what I am, but can't help wanting to be myself,
though it's hard to accept the unacceptable.

I lack the will-power for self-discipline –
get carried away – like a canoe over the rapids.

Beauty, for me, is not a monotype.
Incentives to love are legion.

Shyness, for instance, firing imagination
makes downcast eyes my downfall.

I admire the poise of a forward girl
and presume on her lively company in bed.

If she looks severe and unassailably virtuous,
I suspect she wants what she won't admit.

If she's cultured, her trained mind attracts me,
and if she's not, her naivety.

Then there's the fan who prefers me to Callimachus –
of course I become a fan of hers.

And the critic who carps at me and my work –
she needs a lesson in appreciation.

A graceful walk can step into my life.
Awkwardness requires male relaxation.

A silvery soprano tempts me
to steal a coloratura kiss.

If she plays the guitar *con amore*,
her fingers tug at my heart-strings.

The twining arms and swaying hips
of the cabaret dancer

could make Hippolytus priapic
let alone me.

The tall girl over there comes straight from Homer –
Andromache on a *chaise longue*.

Her friend's petite. I find both irresistible –
short or tall they measure up to my dreams.

I admire a girl in make-up for what she is
and a girl without for what she could be.

I love the pale and I love the golden
– the swarthy are lovely too.

Black hair on snow-white shoulders
reminds me of Leda's raven locks,

a platinum blonde of flaxen-haired Aurora.
Love, I find, mythologizes life.

I fall for the young and feel for the not so young –
one has the looks, the other the experience.

Put it like this – there's beauty in Rome to please all tastes
and mine are all-embracing.

Her Unfaithfulness

Cupid, pack up your quiver. Is any love worthwhile
if it makes me long with all my heart for death?

And I long to die, my hell on earth, my darling,
when I think how you deceived me.

No secret notes, no presents smuggled in
laid bare your infidelity.

I only wish I couldn't prove it.
Why oh why is my case so good?

A man's in luck if his girl can say *Not Guilty*
and he can defend her with confidence.

It's callous and vindictive
to fight for a costly verdict against a sweetheart.

But I saw you both, with my own eyes. I was cold sober,
not, as you thought, asleep – though the wine was flowing.

I watched a conspiracy of eyebrows,
a confabulation of nods.

I could hear your eyes and decipher your fingers
and read the proposals you tabled in wine.

None of your innocent remarks escaped me –
the code was obvious.

When all the other guests had gone,
except a few young men, dead to the world,

I saw you kissing one another –
tongues deeply involved.

No sisterly kisses those,
but long and passionate –

the sort Venus gives Mars,
not Diana Phoebus.

'Stop' I shouted. 'That pleasure's mine.
I shall claim my rights.

You and I enjoy them in common.
Third parties are out.'

As I went on angrily speaking my mind
her face turned a guilty red –

red as the sky when Aurora paints it
or a girl first meeting her betrothed

red as a rose among pale lilies
or the harvest moon bewitched

or tinted Lydian ivory
that time never yellows.

Her blush was one of these, or maybe all.
She'd never looked more lovely – unintentionally.

She stared remorsefully at the ground –
remorseful staring suited her.

I felt like pulling her hair (it was perfectly set)
and scratching her eyes out

but when I saw her face my arms fell,
foiled by the feminine.

Anger vanished. I found myself begging
for kisses as good as those I'd watched.

She burst out laughing and treated me to her best –
they'd make an angry Jupiter drop his bolt.

Did the other man have my luck? The thought torments me.
I wish they'd been less good.

They were far better than the ones I taught her –
she must have had extra tuition.

It's a pity they gave me such pleasure,
a pity our tongues ever met,

because now I have two worries: kisses, yes,
but not only kisses.

That sort must have been learnt in bed;
so at least one teacher has been well paid.

The Death of Her Parrot

Parrot is dead – the Indian mimic.
Flock, you birds, to his funeral.

Good birds all, with wings and talons
tear your hackles, beat your breasts.

Rend your feathers in lieu of hair,
in lieu of the trumpet flute your songs.

Ah Philomel, forget the crime of Tereus,
past centuries of lamentation.

Great loss was Itylus, but long ago –
transfer your tears to a rare contemporary.

All feathered aeronauts must weep for him,
especially his friend the turtledove.

They lived in full agreement,
faithful and true to the end,

Turtle the Pylades
to Parrot's brief Orestes.

But what avail devotion,
gorgeous colours, versatile voice,

Corinna's constant love? Alas
here lies Parrot, paragon of birds.

Greener his feathers than the brittle emerald,
his beak purple, with saffron spots.

Bird-master of impersonation
he was uniquely articulate.

But Fate, in envy, took him,
the prophet of non-violence

whose tastes were ascetic, whose love of talk
left little time for large meals.

Nuts were his diet, poppyseed his sleeping pills,
his drink plain water.

Aggressive quails reach riper years –
perhaps because their life is struggle.

Voracious vultures, circling kites,
rainmaker jackdaws, all live long

Minerva's bugbear the carrion crow
can survive nine human generations.

But Parrot is dead, humanity's echo,
the talking gift from the Far East.

Fate always picks on the best first
and allows the worst to stay the course.

Thersites watched Protesilaus die,
and Hector was ashes long before his brothers.

I skip Corinna's anxious prayers –
a storm-wind blew them away.

On the seventh day, the day of doom,
Destiny stood with empty distaff.

But weak as he was he could still speak,
and his last words were *Goodbye, Corinna.* –

Under a hill in Elysium, a grove of black ilex grows,
and the ground is ever moist and green.

There, to the eye of faith, is the good birds' heaven,
barred to all birds of prey.

Harmless swans feed there at large
with the long-lived solitary phoenix.

Peacocks give spontaneous displays,
and amorous doves kiss and coo.

They have welcomed Parrot to a perch of honour
and applaud his pious ejaculations.

His bones lie decently buried, in a tomb as large as himself,
where a miniature headstone bears this brief inscription:

IN LOVING MEMORY OF POLLY,
A HIGHLY EDUCATED BIRD.

His Self-defence

So that's my role – the professional defendant?
I'm sick of standing trial – though I always win.

At the theatre I've only to glance at the back rows
and your jealous eye pin-points a rival.

A pretty girl need only look at me
and you're sure the look is a signal.

I compliment another woman – you grab my hair.
I criticize her – and you think I've something to hide.

If I'm looking well, I don't love you.
If pale, I'm pining for someone else.

I wish to God I had been unfaithful –
the guilty can take their punishment.

As it is you accuse me blindly, believing anything.
It's your own fault your anger cuts no ice.

Remember the donkey, putting his long ears back –
the more he's beaten the slower he goes.

So that's the latest count against me –
I'm carrying on with your maid Cypassis?

Good God, if I wanted variety
is it likely I'd pick on a drudge like her?

What man of breeding would sleep with a slave
or embrace a body scarred by the lash?

Besides, she's your coiffeuse – her skill
makes her a favourite of yours.

I'd be mad to ask a maid so devoted to you.
She'd only turn me down and tell.

By Venus and Cupid's bow,
I'm innocent – I swear it!

He Blackmails the Coiffeuse

Cypassis, incomparable coiffeuse
who should start a *salon* on Olympus,

no country lass, as I know from our encounters,
but Corinna's treasure and my treasure-hunt –

who was it told her about *us*?
How does she know we slept together?

I didn't blush though, did I? Said nothing by mistake
to betray our secret?

I may have argued no one in his right mind
would have an affair with a maid,

but Achilles adored his maid Briseis
and Agamemnon fell for his slave Cassandra.

I can't claim to be greater than those two.
What goes for royalty is good enough for me.

Corinna looked daggers at *you* though.
And how you blushed! I saw you.

But I saved the day, you must admit,
by swearing my Venus oath.

– Dear goddess, bid the warm south winds
blow that white lie over the ocean! –

So in return, my black beauty,
reward me today with your sweet self.

Why shake your head? The danger's over.
Don't be ungrateful. Remember your duty to *me*.

If you're stupid enough to refuse I'll have to confess
and betray myself for betraying her.

I'll tell your mistress where and when we met, Cypassis,
and what we did and how many times and how we did it.

Time to Give Up Love

Cupid, contempt's far more than you deserve
for loafing about in my heart.

Why pick on me? Have I ever deserted your colours?
Why am I wounded in my own camp?

Is it always friends your torch and arrows pierce and burn?
There'd be more glory in overcoming resistance.

Remember Achilles – who healed the wound
his spear gave Telephus.

No sportsman shoots at a sitting target – and after a kill
he presses on, following a fresh trail.

But opponents never feel your strength – it's we who suffer,
we the army of your faithful.

Thanks to you I'm little more than a skeleton –
why blunt the barbs of your arrows on bare bones?

There are so many looking for love, so many men and women
waiting for your day of glory.

Rome would still be a village of thatched huts
if she hadn't used her power to conquer the world.

The old soldier settles down on his small-holding,
the old race-horse enjoys the run of the woodland pasture,

ships of the line are laid up in dry dock,
gladiators exchange the sword for a harmless foil:

long service on love's active list has earned me my discharge
– it's high time I took life easy.

But He Can't Face It

Offered a sexless heaven I'd say *No thank you* –
women are such sweet hell.

Of course one gets bored, and passion cools, but always
desire begins to spiral again.

Like a horse bolting, with helpless rider
tugging at the reins,

or a gust catching a yacht about to tie up
and driving her out to sea,

Cupid's erratic air-stream hits me,
announcing love's target practice.

Then shoot, boy! I can't resist you.
Your aim strikes home in my heart.

Love's missiles lodge there automatically now –
they hardly know your quiver.

I pity the man whose idea of bliss
is eight hours' sleep.

Poor fool – what's sleep but death warmed up?
Resting in peace comes later.

Lead me astray, beguiling female voices.
Feed me on hope,

cooing today, cursing tomorrow,
locking me out and letting me in.

The fortunes of love. Cupid, Mars takes after you –
like stepson, like stepfather.

You're unpredictable, far more flighty than your wings,
giving delight, denying delight, evading questions.

But maybe you and your lovely mother will hear this prayer:
be king of my heart for ever,

let women, those floating voters, crowd into the kingdom
and both sexes join there in your worship.

In Love with Two Girls at Once

Graecinus, I blame *you*. Yours that memorable remark
'No one can love two girls at once'.

I trusted you and dropped my guard. The result
is too embarrassing – a double love-life.

They're both beautiful, both sophisticated.
It's hard to say which has more to offer.

Certainly one is more attractive – but which one?
I love each more than either,

torn by a schizophrenic passion,
a catamaran in contrary winds.

Great Aphrodite, one girl's hell enough on earth –
why double-damn me?

Why add leaves to trees, stars to the Milky Way,
water to the deep blue sea?

Still, two loves are better than none at all.
God send my enemies a moral life,

single sleep and limbs relaxed
in mid-mattress.

But give *me* ruthless love – to interrupt my slumbers
with company in bed.

Let woman be my undoing – one, if one's enough –
otherwise two.

I can take it. I may be thin and underweight
but I've muscle and stamina.

Pleasure's a food that builds me up.
I've never disappointed a girl.

Many's the night I've spent in love
and been fighting fit the morning after.

To die in love's duel – what final bliss!
It's the death I should choose.

Let soldiers impale their hearts on a pike
and pay down blood for glory,

Let seafaring merchants make their millions
till they and their lies are shipwrecked at last.

But when *I* die let me faint in the to and fro of love
and fade out at its climax.

I can just imagine the mourners' comment:
'Death was the consummation of his life.'

The Send-off

Pines from the peak of Pelion started it –
Argo staggering the waves

in a reckless dash through the Clashing Rocks
to find and win the famous Fleece.

If only she'd sunk in those wild waters
and sea-going ships were unknown!

But now it's Corinna, leaving the shelter of home and bed
to go on a treacherous voyage.

Darling, why make me afraid of winds from east and west,
from icy north and spicy south?

Are there woodland walks or city splendours
in the cruel, blue, monotonous sea?

Delicate shells and coloured pebbles
are treasure-trove of the foreshore.

Beauty should walk the beach with shining feet;
beyond the water's edge lies danger.

Let others tell you of tempests and tornadoes,
Charybdis' rock and Scylla's cave,

the stormy cliffs of Thunder Mountain,
the Libyan quicksands.

Believe what you hear. No storm can harm
a true believer.

Too late to look back when the rope's cast off
and your freighter heads for the far horizon,

when the captain scans the sky for squalls
and sees death as near as the water.

How pale you'll turn
if Triton sets the waves tossing!

How hard you'll pray to Leda's twins,
and how you'll envy people ashore!

It's far safer to put your feet up
and read a book or strum the guitar.

Still, if I'm wasting words on the winds
may Galatea do her level best for you.

On your heads be it, Nereids and father Nereus,
if such a girl is lost for ever.

Think of me, love, on the voyage out, and race home
with a stronger breeze filling the canvas,

wind and tide set fair for Italy,
Nereus tilting the sea this way.

Ask and the western airs shall blow.
Trim the sails with your own hands.

Down on the beach I'll be the first
to sight the ship that brings my idol.

I'll carry you ashore – smother you with kisses –
lay the promised victim low.

We'll make a couch of soft sand
with a dune for table

and over the wine you'll spin me yarns
of giant waves that nearly drowned you,

of white squalls and black nights
and how you weren't afraid – because of me.

Invent it all, if you like. Your fiction shall be fact
and truth my heart's desire.

Oh bring me that day, bright Lucifer!
Bring it me soon – at full gallop.

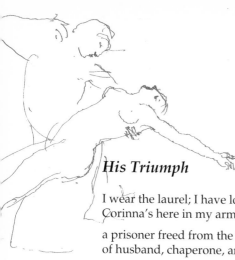

His Triumph

I wear the laurel; I have loved and won.
Corinna's here in my arms,

a prisoner freed from the Triple Alliance
of husband, chaperone, and door,

a prize of war, won without bloodshed,
ready for the Grand Victory Parade;

no mere defensive position with breastworks and a ditch,
but a live girl. There's leadership for you!

When Troy, besieged for a decade, fell at last,
it was little credit to Agamemnon.

But in this one-man operation
the kudos is all mine,

as commander and commanded,
as horse, and foot, and standard-bearer,

whose master plan eliminated luck
and achieved success by devotion to beauty.

Nor is the *casus belli* new:
two continents fought for Helen;

Centaurs and Lapiths brawled
at Hippodamia's wedding;

Trojans waged war again
in Latium for Lavinia;

Sabines in Rome's infancy
fought to win back their women.

It's animal nature. I've seen two bulls battling for a heifer,
spurred on by her big brown eyes.

I am only one of Cupid's many campaigners,
bearing his standard, but avoiding bloodshed.

She Attempts Abortion

My foolish love, being pregnant, tried to end it
and now she lies at death's door.

How could she take that risk without telling me?
I ought to be angry but I'm only afraid.

Still, the child was mine, or at least I think so.
I'm apt to assume what's possible is fact.

O Isis, queen of Paraetonium and lush Canopus,
of Memphis and the palm-groves of Pharos,

and where the broad fast-flowing Nile
runs into the sea through seven mouths,

I beseech you by your sistrum, by Anubis' jackal head
(so may Osiris ever love your mysteries,

the sleepy snake slide round your treasure-chambers,
and the bull-god Apis follow your processions)

look down from heaven upon us and save two lives in one –
for hers depends on you and mine on her.

She has devoutly kept your days of supplication,
sitting where eunuch priests dip your sacred laurel,

and you are known to have compassion
on the heavy bodies of women in labour.

O Isis Ilithyia, hear my prayer, have mercy
and let her live, for she deserves your kindness.

And I shall wear white linen and burn incense on your altar
and lay my promised gifts at your feet,

recording thanks in stone for Corinna's safety
if only you will make it possible. –

This may be no time for advice, darling,
but never again risk your life in that mortal duel.

He Argues Against It

Why should girls be exempt from war-service
and refuse to follow the Amazons

if they carry lethal weapons in peace-time
and suffer self-inflicted wounds?

The first woman to tear an embryo from the womb
should have died of that assault herself.

How can you fight this duel on the sands of death
simply to save your stomach a few wrinkles?

If the mothers of old had followed your vicious example
mankind would be extinct –

we should need a second Deucalion
to renew our stony stock.

Who would have broken the power of Priam
had Thetis cut short her pregnancy?

Had Ilia murdered her unborn twins
who would have founded the queen of cities?

The world could wait in vain for Caesar
if Venus miscarried with Aeneas.

You yourself would have died unbeautiful
had your own mother been callous as you.

And is it not better for me to die of love
than be murdered by my mother?

Why rob the vine when the grapes are growing?
Why strip the tree of bitter fruit?

Let it ripen, ready to fall. Let first beginnings be.
New life is worth a little patience.

Why jab the needle in your own flesh
and poison the unborn?

We condemn Medea and Philomela
for murdering their children –

both were inhuman mothers: but both had bitter cause
to punish their men by such blood-sacrifice.

Is there a Jason or is there a Tereus driving you
to mutilate your own body?

No tigress in wild Armenia does that –
no lioness destroys her own cubs.

But tender-hearted girls do – and pay the penalty:
for the murderess often dies herself,

dies and is carried out in a shroud of hair to the burning,
and the people who see it shout *Serve her right*!

May my words vanish on the wind
and bring us no bad luck.

May the gods be gracious, overlook a first offence
and give her a second chance.

The Signet-ring

Signet-ring, tenant elect of a pretty girl's finger,
whose real value is the giver's love,

I wish you a warm welcome, and immediate installation
behind her second knuckle.

Fit her as snugly as she fits me,
gently hugging her finger.

Lucky you to be drawn on by my darling!
You make me jealous.

O for my metamorphosis into a ring,
by some desert island witch, or sea wizard!

Then, when I wanted to slip a hand inside her dress
and touch her breast,

I should squeeze my way off her finger
and drop by magic into her brassière.

Or suppose she was sealing a love-letter:
to stop the wax sticking to the stone

she'd kiss me first, with the tip of her tongue –
let's hope I shouldn't be sealing my own fate.

When she wanted to put me away, I'd refuse to move,
contracting, clinging tighter.

But I'd never embarrass you, darling,
or burden that delicate finger.

Wear me when you have a bath, and don't worry
if water seeps under the stone.

When you undress, I fancy my setting will rise
and I'll show you a phallic facet.

Fantastic thought. – Go to her, little gift,
and prove my love is genuine.

Alone at Sulmona

Here I am at Sulmona, one of the Pelignian ridings,
small and fresh, a land of streams.

Even in the heat of July, when the parched earth cracks
and the Dog Star glitters,

there are clear waters winding through the Pelignian fields,
keeping them soft and green.

Wheat does well in this fine soil, the vine even better;
there are olive groves too

and deep meadow pastures, with loitering brooks
overhung by long grasses.

Still, my flame isn't here – or rather there's fire in my heart,
but the fire-raiser is far away.

Offered a place between Castor and Pollux,
I'd refuse heaven to be with her.

A troubled sleep in graves of clay
to the men who cut the world into roads.

If the world *had* to be cut up, they should have decreed
that lovers always travel together.

Then, as I tramped the wind-swept Alps,
my girl would make the going good.

With her I'd put to sea in a gale,
force my way through Libyan sandbanks,

laugh at the hell-hounds in Scylla's womb,
at the perils of Cape Malea,

and all the sunken wrecks
in Charybdis' whirlpool.

If Neptune's fury overwhelmed us,
sweeping away our guardian gods,

with her snow-white arms around me
I'd easily bear my lovely burden

remembering how Leander swam across to Hero,
safe, till the night her lamp was darkened.

But without you, darling, here among rows of vines
and brimming streams,

where the peasant sings as he opens the sluices
and a cool air rustles the olive leaves,

it's as though I'm not at Sulmona
on the farm where I was born,

but far away in Scythia, wild Cilicia, woad-painted Britain,
or perched on Prometheus' murderous crag.

Elm loves vine, vine clings to elm –
why are we two so often parted?

You promised never to leave me, swore it on my life
by those twin stars your eyes.

But a woman's word is lighter than a leaf falling,
floating away on the wind or the water.

If in your heart you pity my loneliness,
don't promise – act.

Harness the Gallic ponies and race here in the trap,
cracking the whip over their flying manes,

and the roads in the winding valleys will straighten out for you,
and the high mountains level down as you pass.

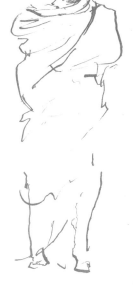

A Woman's Slave

It's immoral, you say, to be a woman's slave?
All right then – label me an immoralist.

I'd welcome disgrace if only the island goddess
would show me cool consideration.

If I was fated to fall for beauty
couldn't my beautiful fate be kind?

But beauty is proud – beauty makes Corinna hard.
Alas she knows herself too well,

prides herself on daily reflection,
the blinkered study of her make-up.

O beauty, born to hold my gaze,
although you reign in Beauty's right

you wrong me by disdain.
Can't greatness condescend?

Calypso fell in mortal love –
kept a reluctant man.

Peleus slept with a Nereid,
Numa with a Naiad.

Vulcan limps from his anvil
home to bed with Venus.

Six syllables and five
can make a couplet .

So take me, love – on any terms.
Lay down the law in bed.

I shan't disgrace you, and you'd miss me.
We never need disown our love.

My capital is balanced couplets.
Women apply to me for credit.

I know your would-be namesake –
she'd pay me to be you.

But Padus and Eurotas
run separate ways for ever,

and I shall always be *your* poet,
and you alone my theme.

His Latest Poetry

While you continue your epic advance on Achilles' wrath
and arm the heroes who swore to avenge Menelaus,

I am defaulting, Macer, in the shady walks of love,
where Cupid shatters my high-poetic hopes.

I keep telling my girl it's all over between us
and next moment find her in my lap.

I say I'm ashamed of myself and she retorts in tears
'But not, surely, of loving little me?'

Then she flings her arms round my neck and gives me
a thousand demoralizing kisses.

That finishes me. Seconded from the field of epic
I report on the home front and war between the sexes.

Lately, though, I grasped the sceptre and wrote a tragedy,
finding the genre suited my genius,

but Cupid laughed at my royal robes and red leather boots
and the sceptre I'd usurped so rashly,

and once again I bowed to the will of a jealous woman –
Love triumphant over the tragic bard.

So now I do what I can — lecture in verse on the art of love,
exposing myself to attack by my own pupils –

or write love-letters – Penelope to Ulysses,
a *cri de cœur* from deserted Phyllis,

mail for ungrateful Jason, for Macareus and Paris,
for Theseus and his son Hippolytus,

a monologue from poor Dido holding a sword,
another from Sappho holding her Lesbian lyre.

How quickly my friend Sabinus returned from his world-tour
and brought back replies from distant addresses!

Penelope can recognize Ulysses' writing;
Phaedra reads a note from her stepson;

Aeneas, dutiful once more, replies to unhappy Dido,
and Phyllis, were she alive, could hear from Demophoon;

a cruel letter from Jason reaches Hypsipyle;
Sappho feels loved and presents her lyre to Phoebus.

Even you, dear Macer, saving your epic dignity,
sing of golden love in wartime,

of Paris and Helen, faithless but world-famous,
of Laodamia, faithful unto death.

I'm sure these suit your book far better than battles.
You'll soon be posted as an epic deserter.

An Appeal to Her Husband

Guard your girl, stupid – if only to please *me*.
I want to want her more.

I'm bored by what's allowed, what isn't fascinates me.
Love by another man's leave is too cold-blooded.

Lovers need a co-existence of hope and fear –
a few disappointments help us to dream.

I write off beautiful women who won't bother to deceive me.
I can't love what never turns nasty.

Corinna, clever girl, noticed this weakness of mine
and knew the best way to exploit it.

Sometimes she'd invent a headache
and tell me to clear off,

sometimes she'd say she'd been unfaithful
and look as if she really had.

Then, having fanned my fading passion to a blaze,
she'd be sweet again and exquisitely obliging.

What irresistible temptation she could offer,
and oh my God the artistry of her kisses!

You too, latest and dearest, must learn to look alarmed
and master the art of saying No.

Let me lie full length on your doorstep
all frosty night long,

and my love will last, growing stronger as time passes –
that's the way to keep passion in training.

Love on a plate soon palls –
like eating too much cake.

Danaë unconfined
would have missed her famous confinement.

Io as a heifer
doubled her human charm.

If you want what's easy to get, pick leaves off trees,
drink Tiber water,

but if you want your power to last, deceive your lover.
Perhaps I'll live to regret that advice,

but come what may it's cruel to be too kind.
If you want to be chased you must run away.

As for you, sir, Beauty's blissful ignoramus,
start locking up at nightfall,

ask about those taps on the door,
the dogs barking in the small hours,

all those notes the maid delivers,
and why the mistress wants to sleep alone.

Become concerned. Allow suspicion to prey on you
and give me a chance to show my skill.

An affair with the wife of a fool
is stealing sand from the beach.

I'm warning you: start guarding your girl
or I'll stop wanting her.

I've suffered long enough – in the vain hope
you'd take precautions so I could take advantage.

But you won't react like a normal husband
and I can't make love on sufferance.

Shall I never be locked out
or face reprisals one fine night?

Never be scared? Never insomniac or sad?
Can't you give me some excuse for wishing you dead?

I don't approve of uncomplaining, pimping husbands –
their immorality ruins my pleasure.

Find someone who can appreciate your perversion,
or, if you value *me* as a rival, use your veto.

BOOK THREE

Two Formidable Ladies

An ancient wood, for many years unlopped by the axe,
haunted, one felt, by an unseen presence.

In the middle a cave, arching over a sacred spring,
and everywhere the plaintive singing of birds.

I was strolling here, in leafy twilight,
wondering what my next poem should be,

when Elegy appeared, her perfumed hair swept-up,
and one foot shorter, I think, than the other.

The fault was oddly attractive, She had style,
an elegant ensemble, a loving look.

Tragedy followed, a stormy figure, striding along,
hair over furrowed brow, mantle trailing,

wearing high Lydian boots and holding a sceptre
imperiously in her left hand.

'Poet' she exclaimed 'haven't you finished with love yet?
Aren't you tired of that tiresome subject?

Your escapades are the talk of every drunken party
and every back-street corner.

People stare and point at you as you walk past –
"That's him" they say, "there goes Cupid's firework."

Those indecent exposés of your private life
have made you a Roman scandal – and you can't see it.

It's time you felt the full weight of Bacchus' rod.
Stop shirking. Start a major work.

Your talent needs more scope: great men and their achievements –
that, you'll find, is your proper field.

So far you've thrown off some pretty lyrics for the girls,
but the time for juvenilia is over.

Roman Tragedy waits for you to make her famous –
for your vitality to satisfy her needs.'

At this, bolt upright in those high red boots,
she nodded four times, tossing her thick hair.

Elegy – armed, I think, with a myrtle wand –
smiled at her maliciously.

'Pompous creature!' she said. 'You and your moralizing!
Can't you ever be light-hearted?

Thank you for condescending to preach in couplets –
for attacking me in my own metre.

I have no wish to aspire to your sublime.
Your palace dwarfs my little door.

I'm light and frivolous, like my darling Cupid –
as unheroic as my theme.

But without me Venus would be vulgar –
she needs me as mentor and manager.

The door your high boot can't kick open
opens wide to my sweet words.

I taught Corinna to trick her minder
and tamper with trusty locks,

to slip out of bed in her nightdress
and tiptoe through the dark.

My power is greater than yours because I've suffered –
things your pride could never endure.

Many's the time I've been pinned against a locked door
and braved the stares of passers-by.

What's more I remember hiding in a maid's dress
till the chaperone was out of the way.

I've even been torn apart and plunged in water
when I went as birthday present to that illiterate girl.

It was I who awakened your poetic gift;
it's thanks to me this woman is after you now.'

'Goddesses both' I hesitated, 'please listen.
I'm anxious not to offend either.

One of you does me the honour of high boots and a sceptre.
She has touched my tongue – I can feel my diction rising.

The other offers my love a name that will live . . .
Well . . . the long and the short of it is – I choose her.

Grant your bard a breathing-space, Tragedy.
You need endless time and trouble. What *she* wants is short.'

The goddess relented. Hurry along there, Amorini.
Time presses. At my back I can sense a masterpiece.

At the Races

It's not the horses that bring me here
though I hope your favourite wins.

To sit with you and talk with you is why I've come –
I've come to tell you I'm in love.

If I watch you and you watch the races
we'll both enjoy watching a winner.

How I envy your charioteer!
He's a lucky man to be picked by you.

I wish it was me. I'd get my team
off to a flying start,

crack the whip, give them their heads
and shave the post with my nearside wheel.

But if I caught sight of *you* in the race
I'd drop the reins and lose ground.

Poor Pelops was nearly killed at Pisa
gazing in Hippodamia's eyes,

but being her favourite of course he won
as I hope your driver and I will. –

It's no good edging away. The line brings us together –
that's the advantage of the seating here.

You on the right, sir – please be careful.
Your elbow's hurting the lady.

And you in the row behind – sit up, sir!
Your knees are digging into her back.

My dear, your dress is trailing on the ground.
Lift it up – or there you are, I've done it for you.

What mean material to hide those legs!
Yes, the more one looks the meaner it seems.

Legs like Atalanta,
Milanion's dream of bliss.

A painter's model for Diana
running wilder than the beasts.

My blood was on fire before. What happens now?
You're fuelling a furnace, flooding the Red Sea.

I'm sure that lightweight dress is hiding
still more delightful revelations.

But what about a breath of air while we wait?
This programme will do as a fan.

Is it really as hot as I feel? Or merely my imagination
fired by your sultry presence?

Just then a speck of dust fell on your white dress.
Forgive me – out, damned spot!

But here's the procession. Everybody hush.
Give them a hand. The golden procession's here.

First comes Victory, wings outstretched.
Goddess, grant me victory in love!

Neptune next. Salute him, sailors.
Not for me the ocean – I'm a landlover.

Soldiers, salute Mars. I'm a disarmer,
all for peace and amorous plenty.

There's Phoebus for the soothsayers. Phoebe for the hunters,
Minerva for the master craftsmen.

Farmers can greet Bacchus and Ceres,
boxers pray to Pollux and knights to Castor.

But I salute the queen of love and the boy with the bow.
Venus, smile on my latest venture.

Make my new mistress willing – or weak-willed.
A lucky sign – the goddess nodded

giving her promise. And now I'm asking for yours.
With Venus' permission I'll worship *you*.

By all these witnesses, divine and human,
I swear I want you to be mine for ever.

But the seat's a bit too high for you.
Why not rest your feet on the railing in front?

Now, they've cleared the course. The Praetor's starting the first race.
Four-horse chariots. Look – they're off.

There's your driver. Anyone *you* back is bound to win.
Even the horses seem to know what you want.

My God, he's taking the corner too wide.
What are you doing? The man behind is drawing level.

What are you doing, wretch? Breaking a poor girl's heart.
For pity's sake pull on your left rein!

We've backed a loser. Come on everyone, all together,
flap your togas and signal a fresh start.

Look, they're calling them back. Lean your head against me
so the waving togas don't disarrange your hair.

Now, they're off again – plunging out of the stalls,
rushing down the course in a clash of colours.

Now's your chance to take the lead. Go all out for that gap.
Give my girl and me what we want.

Hurrah, he's done it! You've got what you wanted, sweetheart.
That only leaves me – do I win too?

She's smiling. There's a promise in those bright eyes.
Let's leave now. You can pay my bet in private.

Her Perjury and the Gods

Gods? There are none.
Or how could she break her solemn oath and keep her beauty?

Her waist-long hair is as long today
as before she flouted the Almighty.

In her face the lily and the rose
are glowing still – snow-white, pale red.

Her feet are still small and slender,
her figure lithe and lovely.

Her flashing eyes still shine like stars
though forsworn so often. –

Of course. Beauty is divine. Even the deathless gods
forgive a lovely woman's lies.

Lately she swore an oath, by the eyes of both of us,
but mine were the ones to suffer.

Great Gods, if you forgive her perjuries
why make me pay for them?

Is it not shame enough you ordered Andromeda
to die for the sin of her ugly mother?

Is it not shame enough you ignored my cry for help
and let her fool us both and laugh about it?

Can she also redeem her deceit at my expense? Must I
doubly deceived stand in for my deceiver? –

Either God is an empty word, a false terror
to overawe the credulous crowd,

or if he exists he's in love with the girls
and surrenders omnipotence to them.

Against us men Mars buckles on his blade
and Pallas hurls her spear.

Against us men Apollo bends his bow
and Jupiter aims his bolt.

But slighted Gods are afraid to offend the girls –
Beauty's assurance terrifies them.

Then why bother to burn incense?
We men should show more spirit.

Jupiter's lightning strikes his own high places
but he takes good care to miss the perjured sex.

When thousands deserved his bolt only poor Semele
went up in flames – killed for being kind.

Yet had she refused her lover
his maternal side would never have developed. –

But why complain? Why hurl abuse at the pantheon?
Gods too have eyes, Gods too have tender hearts.

If I were God I'd give the girls a licence
to lie and take my name in vain.

As a broad-minded Olympian
I'd even swear they'd sworn truly.

But, sweetheart, don't abuse your divine right
or in future at least go easy on my eyes.

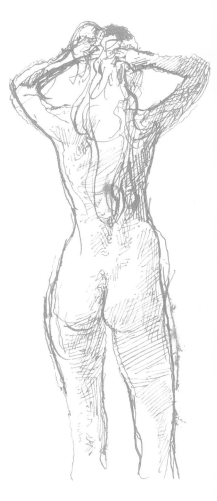

Vice and Veto

It's no good guarding a pretty girl, you big bully.
Her own instinct ought to protect her.

The chastity of fear is fake,
and forced refusal a form of consent.

However strictly you guard her body her thoughts can lust.
You can't imprison a woman's will.

With all your locks you can't even guard her body –
she'll find a lover among the household.

If you let her sin she'll be less of a sinner.
Responsibility takes the kick out of free love.

If I were you I shouldn't encourage vice by veto;
you'll find concession a stronger deterrent.

The other day I watched a horse on a tight rein –
he took the bit between his teeth and bolted,

but stopped dead the moment he felt the reins relax
and drop loose on his flying mane.

We're all rebels against restriction – in love with the illicit –
sick men craving the fluid they're forbidden.

Argus had eyes in the back of his head – hundreds of them,
but Cupid tricked him single-handed.

Into her bower of stone and steel Danaë entered
virginal – to emerge a mother.

But Penelope kept faith without a guard
among that crowd of young suitors.

Locked up means more desirable. Security
is a challenge to thieves. Few can love by another man's leave.

Your wife's beauty is less of a draw than your passion for her –
she's got something special, we think, to hold you.

By being possessive you make her more worthwhile as a mistress;
in fact her fear counts for more than her figure.

Storm as you please, forbidden fruit is sweet.
The woman who says 'I daren't' is the one for me.

However, you've no right to imprison a free-born girl.
Such sanctions are for foreigners only.

And her warder will say it's thanks to him. Do you want a slave
to take the credit for her chastity?

To fret about adultery is too provincial
and shows ignorance of Roman manners –

after all, the Martian twins were born out of wedlock,
Ilia's children, Romulus and Remus.

Why marry good looks if all you wanted was good behaviour?
The two things never mix.

Be sensible and give in to her. Stop being a prig.
Don't press your rights as a husband,

but cultivate the many friends she'll bring you.
You'll reap a rich reward for doing nothing,

go out when you like to all the liveliest parties,
or stay at home and enjoy the presents you never gave her.

The Dream

'I was tired that night and sleep came soon
bringing a dreadful dream.

I dreamt of a grove of ilex, under a sunny hill,
alive with birds among the leaves,

and a green meadow where the trees ended,
and a murmuring of water.

I was sheltering from the heat, there in the shade of the leaves
– though the leafy shade gave little shelter –

when a white heifer looking for sweet grasses and flowers
halted in front of me.

Whiter than snow she was
when it lies new-fallen,

whiter than sheep's milk at milking time
when it froths in the pail.

A bull, her happy mate, followed
and lay down at her side,

lay there peacefully feeding,
slowly chewing the cud

till sleep relaxed his powerful neck
and his heavy head sank to the ground.

Then a carrion crow glided down
landing with a loud caw,

pecked the heifer's breast three times and flew away
with a tuft of snow-white hair in her beak.

The heifer at long last abandoned mate and meadow
(her breast now marked with a black bruise)

and seeing bulls in the distance grazing
(there were several grazing in the green distance)

hurried over to join them
in hope of richer grass.

Now tell me, my unknown interpreter of dreams,
if dreams have meaning what does this one mean?'

The interpreter weighed my words
and gave me this reply:

'The heat you tried in vain to avoid
under the restless leaves was love.

The heifer your girl – snow-white for purity.
The bull her lover – you.

The carrion crow pecking her breast
a Madam trying to corrupt her.

As the heifer at long last left her mate
so you will be left – in a cold bed.

The bruise on her breast, those black marks,
are the stain of adultery deep in her heart.'

At this interpretation my blood ran cold
and a great darkness covered my eyes.

The River in Spate

Halt, muddy river! Rest awhile among your reeds.
Make way for a lover in a hurry,

for you haven't a bridge, or a chain-ferry,
to take me across without oars.

I remember you as a little stream, easily forded,
hardly deep enough to wet my ankles.

Now you're in spate, swollen by melting snow from the mountain,
swirling along brown and turbid.

Why did I hurry, scanting sleep,
journeying night and day,

to mark time here, without a hope
of setting foot on the far bank?

O for the wings of the hero
who cut off Medusa's head!

O for the flying wagon
that scattered the first seed!

Signs and wonders, poetic lies –
lost in the daylight of the present.

Listen, swollen river: if you want to roll on for ever
roll on within limits.

Your name will be mud if the tale gets round
that you crossed a poet in love.

Rivers should help young lovers –
rivers too have loved.

Inachus turned pale for Melia –
she warmed his chilly bed.

Before the famous fall of Troy
Xanthus fell for Neaera.

Alpheus ran to Syracuse
after his true love Arethusa.

Peneus kidnapped a bride
and smuggled her into Phthia.

Asopus adored Thebe –
Thebe the mother of five girls.

Where are the horns of Achelous?
Broken, by angry Heracles,

not for Calydon, not for all Aetolia,
but for Deianira the one and only.

Rich father Nile, river of seven mouths
guarding the secret of his rising,

couldn't smother with his flood
the flame Evanthe kindled.

Enipeus gave the order *Waters, about turn!*
and, when they turned about, drily embraced Salmonis.

And don't forget the river tumbling down the rocks
by Tivoli's orchards

the river that fell for Ilia, though she was distraught,
tearing her hair in grief, tearing her cheeks in cruel grief,

mourning the sin of Mars and the crime of Amulius,
wandering barefoot in the wilderness.

Impetuous Anio, seeing her, raised his head
from the rushing waters in rough greeting:

'Ilia, daughter of Ilion's kings,
why do you walk forlorn along my banks?

Why do you wander alone, in mourning,
with no white headband to bind your hair?

Why do you weep and dim those melting eyes with tears
and lacerate your lovely breasts?

Flint-hearted, steely-fleshed is he
who sees your tears and feels no pity.

Ilia, don't be afraid. My palace is waiting for you.
My waters will pay you homage. Ilia, don't be afraid.

You shall be queen of a hundred nymphs – or more,
for a hundred or more live in my stream.

Oh Trojan princess, don't disdain me
but find fulfilment – richer than I've promised.'

She dared not look up to answer;
the warm tears were raining down.

She tried to escape, but couldn't move from the river bank.
Fear had robbed her of strength to run.

Trembling, tearing her hair,
she spoke at last – these bitter words:

'Would I had died a virgin
and lay in my father's tomb!

Why am I offered the torch of marriage –
a Vestal who broke her vows, an outcast of Vesta's flame?

Why live on to be pointed at by vulgar fingers?
Death to the face that shame has branded.'

So saying she held her stole in front of her eyes
and threw herself in the rushing torrent.

But the king of the river slid his hands under her breasts
and made her his queen consort. –

You too, I suppose, have warmed to a woman's flesh,
but these woods conceal your wicked ways.

While I've been talking your waters have spread wider –
your channel isn't deep enough to hold them.

What makes you so wild against me – delaying my delight,
rudely breaking my journey?

It might be different if you were on the map,
a genuine river, known to the world:

but you're a nameless inundation,
a vagrant of no fixed source,

rising in rains and melting snows,
the idle wealth of winter.

In December a muddy torrent,
a dust bath in July

without a drop to wet a traveller's whistle
or earn a beggar's blessing.

In spate a loss to cattle, and a greater loss to crops –
though it's my loss that matters now.

I must have been crazy telling you tales of rivers in love.
I'm ashamed to have dropped the names

of Inachus and Nile and Achelous
in front of such a nondescript.

Mean and muddy torrent, I wish you all you deserve:
drought in winter, and in summer – heat waves.

Impotent

No, I must face facts:
she was lovely – she was glamorous – I was mad about her.

But there I lay, with this girl in my arms, and nothing happened.
The position was absurd.

I wanted it badly enough, and so did she –
but could I rise to the occasion?

Ivory-smooth her arms embraced me –
whiter than snow in sunshine.

Thigh to thigh she kissed me –
deep kisses, alive with desire –

whispered temptation, called me lord and master,
ran through the erotic rosary.

But my body was paralyzed
as though I had drunk hemlock –

lying there like a lay figure.
Was it really me – or my ghost?

So much for fine upstanding youth. And when I grow old –
if I grow old – what then?

Youth and virility – what humiliation!
For all she could tell I had neither.

She left the bed like one of Vesta's nuns
or a sister from her little brother's side.

But the other day I took Chlide twice,
Pitho three times, Libas three,

and as for Corinna – she inspired my record:
in one short night I counted nine.

Could some witch have laid me under a spell?
Given me a magical decoction?

Moulded my image in red wax
and stuck pins in its guts?

Magic can turn a wheat-field into weed,
drain well-springs dry,

make grapes and chestnuts drop,
strip fruit trees bare.

Couldn't it also emasculate muscle?
Yes, it was probably witchcraft –

that, and humiliation too –
aggravating the collapse.

God, what a lovely girl! But I just gazed and clung –
close as a brassière to her breasts.

Her touch could have made a Nestor young again,
resurrected a Tithonus.

Perfection was in my grasp – and a sham in hers.
What have I left to pray for?

The gods must surely regret the gift
I used so badly.

I wanted a welcome – and got it. To kiss her – and I did.
Be alone with her – and I was.

I had all the luck and nothing came of it –
ownership without possession – a miser's million –

Tantalus parched in his pool,
clutching at the unattainable.

I left her pure as the day I was born,
pure enough to enter a temple.

She kissed me high, and she kissed me low –
she tried everything.

She could have moved an oak, softened a stone,
melted adamant,

let alone roused all living men –
but I was neither man nor alive,

and she was Sappho singing to the deaf,
an artist's model posing for the blind.

Though I filled my mind with erotic pictures
and imagined a hundred variations,

I lay there limp and lifeless –
yesterday's drooping rose.

Now of course it's quite different – long and strong,
spoiling for battle, eager to join up.

Lie down, dog!
I've been had like this before.

You tricked me, left me in the lurch,
put me to shame – not to mention expense.

And think of the trouble she took with you –
her delicate handling of my problem.

But you wouldn't budge – not one half-inch.
You took not the slightest notice of her.

'Stop fooling about' she said. 'What's the matter with you?
Who sent you along to lie down here?

Either you've been bewitched
or you've just left another woman.'

With that she leapt out of bed,
barefoot, in a flurry of dressing-gown,

and to prevent the maids from guessing
camouflaged disgrace with a little water.

Money Rules

Does anyone these days respect the artist
or value elegiac verse?

Time was when imagination meant more than money
but today *poor* and *boor* mean the same thing.

'I adore your poetry' she says,
and allows it in where I can't follow.

After the compliments the door curtly closes
and I, her poet, moon about humiliated,

displaced by a new-rich upstart, a bloody soldier
who butchered his way to wealth and a knighthood.

Him in your lovely arms! You in his clutches!
Light of my life, how could you?

That head wore a helmet, remember –
that obliging flank a sword.

His left hand, flashing the new equestrian ring,
once gripped a shield. His right has killed.

How can you hold hands with a killer?
Have you no sensibility?

Look at his scars, marks of a brutal trade –
that body earned him all he has.

I expect he even brags about his killings.
How can you touch him after that, gold-digger,

and allow me, the priest of Phoebus and the Muses,
to serenade your locked door in vain?

No man of taste should waste his time on art –
he'd better enlist and rough it under canvas.

Don't turn out couplets, turn out on parade.
Homer, join up if you want a date!

Jove Almighty realized gold's omnipotence
when he cashed himself to seduce a girl.

Before the transaction father looked grim, daughter prudish,
her turret steely, the doorposts coppered.

But when the crafty lecher arrived in cash
she opened her lap and gave as golden as she got.

Long ago, when Saturn ruled in the kingdom of heaven,
Earth sank all her capital in darkness –

stowed bronze and silver, gold and heavy iron in hell.
Ingots were not yet known:

she had better things to offer – crops without cultivation,
fruit on the bough, honey in the hollow oak.

No one tore the ground with ploughshares
or parcelled out the land

or swept the sea with dipping oars –
the shore was the world's end.

Clever human nature, victim of your inventions,
disastrously creative,

why cordon cities with towered walls?
Why arm for war?

Why take to the sea – as if happiness were far away?
Why not annex the sky too?

We have, in a modest way – by deifying Bacchus
and Hercules and Romulus and now Caesar.

We dig for gold instead of food.
Our soldiers earn blood-money.

The Senate's barred to the poor. Capital is king,
creates the solemn judge and the censorious knight.

Let them own the world – knights controlling Campus and Forum,
Senate dictating peace and war,

but hands off love! Sweethearts shouldn't be up for auction.
Leave the poor man his little corner.

As it is, if my girl were chaste as a Sabine prude
she'd crawl for anyone with money.

So I am locked out. When I'm around she's scared of her husband.
He'd vanish quick enough if I could pay.

O for a god in heaven to right a lover's wrongs
and turn those fat pickings to a pile of dust!

Death of Tibullus

If Thetis and Aurora
Shed tears for their dead sons,
If goddesses feel grief,
Loosen your hair and weep,
Gentle Elegia,
Sorrow's true namesake.
For the spent body of Tibullus
Your poet laureate
Is burning on the tall pyre,
And Cupid's bow is broken,
His quiver reversed,
His torch burnt out.
See how sadly he walks
With wings drooping,
Beating his breast.
And the tears fall
On his wild hair
And he sobs aloud,
As when he left Iulus' palace
Long ago
To follow his brother to the grave.
Venus too grieves for Tibullus
As she grieved for Adonis
When the wild boar ripped his groin.

'Dedicated poet',
'In God's keeping',
'Divinely inspired' – so run the phrases,
But Death mocks dedication
With the laying on
Of invisible hands.
What help were Phoebus and the Muse
To their son Orpheus?
What help the song that tamed wild beasts?
And did not Phoebus in the forest
Sing *Linos ailinos*
To the broken strings of his lyre?
Even Maeonian Homer,
Spring of the water of life
On the lips of poets,
Drowned at last
In black Avernus.
Only his verse evades the pyre,
A rumour of heroic war,
A deceiving web unravelled at night.
His megalith.
So Nemesis and Delia,
Last longing and first love,
Shall be live names,
Though Isis failed them
In a clacking of rattles,

An emptiness of lonely nights.
When evil overtakes the good,
To disbelieve in God
Can be forgiven.
The decent life is death,
The decent worship – death,
Dragging you from high altar to hollow tomb.
Some trust in verse –
Let them look at Tibullus,
A little ash in a little urn.
Flames inspired
And flames destroyed him,
Eating his heart
In desecration
Worse than the gutting
Of a gilded shrine.
And Venus on the heights of Eryx
Looked away –
Hiding the tears perhaps.
But better to die in Rome
Than a stranger on Corfu
Thrust in a cheap grave.
Here at least his mother
Could close the blank eyes
And offer farewell gifts.
His sister could take part

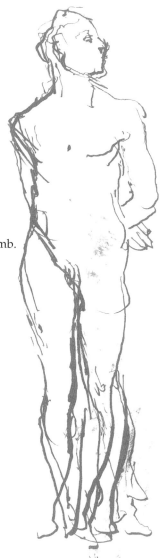

In the ritual of grief,
Tearing dishevelled hair.
Nemesis and his first love
Could attend the pyre
And add their kisses.
'I was the lucky one'
Delia whispered at parting –
'My love gave you life.'
But Nemesis replied
'Not yours the loss.
He died with his hand in mine.'
And yet, if human survival
Is more than a haunting name,
Tibullus lives in Elysium,
Welcomed there by Calvus
And Catullus the scholar-poet,
Young men, ivy-garlanded –
By Gallus too, if the charge
Of friendship betrayed is false,
Gallus who flung away life and love.
To these rare spirits,
If the spirit lives,
Tibullus brings grace.
May his bones rest in peace,
Undisturbed in the urn,
And earth be no burden to his ashes.

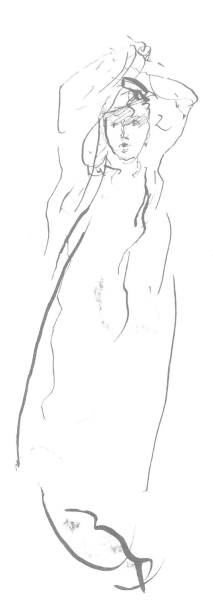

Ceres' Festival

These are the festival days of Ceres –
the nights my love must sleep alone.

Golden goddess, wearing the wheat in your silken hair,
why does your cult say No to pleasure?

Your name is Bountiful among all nations –
no goddess gives more generously.

Long ago, before unshaven peasants parched the corn,
before the threshing-floor was known,

when we lived off the oracular oak
and our food was acorns and a few herbs,

Ceres taught the first seed to sprout in the furrow
and the sickle to cut her yellow hair

and the ox to bend his neck to the yoke
and the plough's tooth to groove the ground.

Can she delight in lovers' tears?
In sackcloth and celibacy?

She's a country goddess but not uncouth –
she too has loved.

Witness Crete – Cretans don't always lie.
Crete was the proud nurse of Jove.

There the ruler of the starry sky
was suckled as a tiny baby.

Crete deserves credit – her foster-son supports her.
She knows the facts and Ceres will plead guilty.

In Crete, below Mount Ida, she saw Iasius
the sure marksman hunting fallow-deer –

saw him and felt the flame leap in her heart.
Shame and desire began their tug of war.

Desire won. A drought cracked the fields
and the crops failed.

Though the crooked share had broken the ground
and heavy mattocks pounded the clods,

though the seed was evenly sown in the furrow,
the farmers were cheated, their prayers unanswered.

Deep in the forest the goddess of fruitfulness dallied
and the grain that crowned her long hair fell off.

Only Crete had abundant crops that year –
it was harvest home wherever the goddess trod.

The woods of Ida grew white with wheat
and the wild boar trampled spelt in the forest.

Lawgiver Minos prayed for more such harvests –
he should have prayed for Ceres' love to last.

Golden goddess, you must have hated sleeping alone.
Then why inflict it on me?

Am I to mourn when your long-lost daughter is found
and reigns as queen, second only to Juno?

Surely a festival calls for wine and woman and song?
Surely these are gifts fit for the gods?

Through with Love

To hell with love! I've been a martyr long enough.
You're quite impossible.

I've slipped my shackles. Yes, I'm now a free man –
I can blush to remember how I forgot myself.

Victory at last. I've planted my foot on Cupid's neck.
I didn't know I had it in me.

'Stick to it' I tell myself, 'don't weaken.
It's painful, but think of the pain as medicine.'

Did I really lie down like a tramp on the pavement
all those nights you locked me out?

Did I really stand guard at your door like a slave
while you were hugging another man?

I well remember seeing your lover leave the house
and stagger home – invalided out.

The worst of it was that he saw me –
I could wish my enemies nothing worse.

Was there a single day when I didn't report for duty
as your personal escort, your friend, your lover?

My company made everybody love you.
My passion for you started a male fashion.

I can't forget the lies you fed me,
the promises you fooled me with,

the nods to lover-boys at parties,
the sly remarks in obvious code.

Once, I heard you were ill, rushed to your house in a panic
and found you in bed – yes, in the arms of my rival.

These and other unspeakable insults have made me hard.
Find someone else to play the martyr.

My ship's in harbour, garlands hanging from the stern,
deaf to the roar of the rising storm.

Don't waste sweet words and bygone witchery on me.
I've learnt some common sense at last.

No, Love Wins

Love and hate, here in my heart, at tug of war –
and love I suppose will find a way to win.

I'd sooner hate. If I can't I'll be the reluctant lover –
the dumb ox bearing the yoke he loathes.

Your behaviour drives me away, your beauty draws me back.
I adore your face and abhor your failings.

With or without you life's impossible
and I can't decide what I want.

Why can't you be less lovely or more true?
Why must your faults and your figure clash?

I love what you are and hate what you do –
but your self, alas, outweighs your selfishness.

By the bed we shared, by all the gods
who let you take their names in vain,

by your face my holy icon, by your eyes that ravished mine,
take pity on me.

Be what you will you'll still be mine – but you must choose –
do you want me to want to love you or be forced to?

Make life plain sailing for me please
by helping me love what I can't help loving.

His Verse Has Made Her Infamous

Did a raven cross my path one day
and croak bad luck on the eternal lover?

Is some malefic planet opposing me?
Have I antagonized a god?

The girl once mine and only mine
is mine alone no longer.

I suppose my poems made her a public figure?
Yes, my flair commercialized her.

And serve me right. I shouldn't have advertised her beauty.
If she's up for sale it's my own fault.

I've been her pimp, procuring lovers for her,
letting them in at the front door.

I doubt the value of verse. It has certainly done me harm,
making people jealous of my success.

In spite of Thebes and Troy and Caesar's victories
my sole inspiration was Corinna.

If only the Muse had frowned on my first efforts
and Phoebus withdrawn his support.

But after all a poem's not an affidavit –
my statements should have been discounted.

We poets thought up Scylla, who stole her father's curl
and kennels hell-hounds in her womb.

We thought up Hermes' winged heels, Medusa's snaky hair,
and Perseus' flying horse.

We elongated that nine-acre giant,
gave Cerberus three heads,

Enceladus a thousand whirling arms.
We spellbound heroes with our Siren voices,

imprisoned the winds in Odysseus' wine-skin,
tormented Tantalus with eternal thirst,

made flint of Niobe, a she-bear of Callisto,
a mournful nightingale of Philomela,

turned Jupiter to feathers and showers of gold
and bulls in the ocean with virgins on their backs.

Add Proteus, and the Theban dragon's teeth,
fire-breathing oxen,

Phaethon's amber-weeping sisters,
ships transformed to nymphs,

the sun in retreat from Atreus' cannibal feast,
and boulders bowling along to the lilt of the lyre.

In short, poetic licence extends to infinity,
but its documents are unhistorical.

My praise of Corinna should have been read as fiction.
You are my trouble – you, uncritical reader.

Juno's Festival

We had come to Falerii, my wife's home,
the orchard town once conquered by Camillus,

and Juno's sisterhood were preparing for her feast –
the crowded games and the sacrifice of a local heifer.

To watch the ritual repays with interest
a trying journey on steep roads.

You reach an ancient grove of thick and gloomy trees
haunted, you feel, by an unseen presence.

Here, at a primitive altar of rough-hewn stone
the faithful offer prayers and incense.

Here, to the music of flutes and plain-chant, every year
a procession comes, through decorated streets

and the crowd's applause, leading snow-white heifers
fattened on Faliscan pasture,

bull calves with danger latent in their foreheads,
pigs – the poor man's offering,

and the lord of the flock, bone-headed, spiral-horned.
Only goats are missing. The goddess hates them.

According to legend, when she ran away from Jove
and hid in the forest a nanny-goat betrayed her.

So now the children throw spears at the tell-tale,
which goes as prize to whoever scores first hit.

Young men and shy girls walk before the goddess,
sweeping the wide street with their trains,

the girls' hair bound with gold and jewels,
their feet gilded, gleaming beneath a stately mantle.

White-robed, in the ancient Greek fashion,
they carry the sacred vessels on their heads,

and the crowd keep silent as Juno passes by
in golden procession behind her sisterhood.

The ritual came from Argos. On Agamemnon's murder
Halaesus fled from his inheritance

and crowned his wanderings over land and sea
by founding these high walls

and teaching his Faliscans the worship of Juno.
May the goddess be gracious – to me and her people, always.

Propriety, Please

Your loveliness, I don't deny, needs lovers,
but spare me facts and figures – please.

My moral code does not require you to be chaste,
but it does demand concealment.

Any woman who pleads Not Guilty is innocent;
only confession gives her a bad name.

What madness to parade your nightlife in the daylight
and publicize your private affairs!

Even prostitutes insist on privacy
and lock the door before obliging a client.

Will *you* expose your naked guilt to scandalmongers
and give full details of your own misconduct?

Have *some* decency, please – or at least pretend to have,
so I can think you're faithful even if you aren't.

Carry on as before, but don't admit it,
and don't be ashamed of decorum in public.

There's a proper place for impropriety –
enjoy it there, shedding your inhibitions.

But don't forget them when you leave.
Confine your faults to bed.

It's no disgrace to undress there,
press thigh to thigh,

kiss as you please, and figure out
love's total variety,

moaning and whispering sweet words,
shaking the bedstead in abandon.

But when you dress put on your moral make-up too
and wear the negative look of virtue.

Take whoever you please – provided you take me in.
Don't enlighten me. Let me keep my illusions.

Need I see those notes coming and going?
That double hollow in the bed?

Your hair in sleepless disarray?
Those love-bites on your neck?

You'll soon be committing adultery before my very eyes.
Destroy your good name if you must, but spare my feelings.

These endless confessions bring me out in a cold sweat –
honestly, they're killing me.

My love becomes frustrated hate for what I can't help loving.
I'd gladly die – if only you'd die with me.

I'll ask no questions, I promise, and ferret out no secrets
if you'll do me the simple favour of deceit.

But if ever I catch you in the act,
if ever I'm forced to see the worst,

then flatly deny I saw what I did,
and your words shall stand in for my eyes.

It's so easy for you to beat a willing loser.
Only remember to say Not Guilty.

Two words can clear you – speak them and win.
Your case may be weak but your judge is weaker.

From Elegy to Tragedy's High Horses

Mother of the Amorini, my couplets race home,
leaving a vacancy,

and I sign myself 'Pelignian Countryman',
'Respectable Rake',

or, if you like, 'Equestrian of the Fourth Generation'
– no jumped-up military knight.

The Mantuans have Virgil, the Veronese Catullus,
but *I* shall be the pride of the Peligni –

freedom-lovers and freedom-fighters
who made imperious Rome afraid.

Picture the future tourist, among these streams,
sizing up Sulmona;

'How tiny to produce a major poet!
I call that great' he'll say.

Child god, and island mother-goddess,
parade your golden banners elsewhere.

The rod of Bacchus reprimands me –
his royal course needs high horses.

Farewell, lively Muse, and unheroic metre,
my labour of love – these immortal remains.

NOTES

The titles of the poems are not authentic but are provided by the translator.

BOOK ONE

11   *second hexameter*: by stealing one of its six feet Cupid turned it into a pentameter (five feet) so that the two lines together formed an elegiac couplet of eleven feet – the usual metre for love poetry.

13   *Augustus*: the *gens Iulia* to which Augustus belonged was named after Iulus, the son of Aeneas, and traced its descent from Venus, mother of Aeneas and Cupid.

23   *Diomede*: the Greek hero who wounded Aphrodite in the hand with his spear when she tried to rescue Aeneas in *Iliad* v.

26   *Penelope*: in *Odyssey* xxi she promises to marry the suitor who can draw Odysseus' bow.

26   *chalk*: slaves newly imported from abroad and on sale in the slave-market had their feet coated with gypsum as a distinguishing mark.

28   *Isis*: the cult of this Egyptian goddess demanded sexual abstinence at certain times of the year.

28   *Via Sacra*: it ran through the Forum and was one of the main shopping centres of ancient Rome.

30   *Rhesus*: the story is told in *Iliad* x.

33   *Tarpeia*: in the time of Romulus she betrayed the Capitol to the Sabines in return for what they carried on their left arms; she meant the gold bracelets they wore, but the Sabines took her to mean their shields and killed her with them.

33   *a necklace*: the necklace of Harmonia, daughter of Mars and Venus, brought death on all its owners. Alcmaeon killed his mother because with it she had been bribed to cause the death of her husband Amphiaraus.

34   *Victory's laurel*: *litterae laureatae* were military dispatches bound with bay to report a victory.

34   *this dedication*: that is, he will turn his writing-tablets into votive tablets.

37   *Memnon*: the Ethiopian, son of Tithonus and Aurora, fought for the Trojans and was killed by Achilles. Every year two troops of birds flew to his tomb in the Troad and fought each other, making a blood-offering to Memnon's ghost.

37   *one-word*: *spondeo* 'I guarantee'.

38   *two nights*: Jupiter spent them with Alcmena, Hercules' mother.

39   *the picture*: the famous Aphrodite Anadyomene of the fourth-century Greek painter Apelles, which Augustus had dedicated in the shrine of Julius Caesar.

40   *German triumph*: Drusus defeated the Sygambri in 11 BC and was allowed an *ovatio* or minor Triumph.

41   This poem celebrates six Greek and eight Latin poets, including Ovid himself, together with a reference to or quotation from the work of each.

NOTES

Book Two

47	*Bagoas*: a Persian name often given to eunuchs.
47	*Danaids*: the portico of Apollo's temple on the Palatine had statues of the fifty daughters of Danaus between its columns.
49	*Poor you . . . good investment*: a separate poem in the MSS.
57	*Thersites*: the ugliest of the Greeks at Troy. Protesilaus was the first of the Greeks to be killed there.
57	*Peacocks*: the Romans believed they had to be praised before they would display their plumage. In the Birds' Paradise they are less vain.
59	*At the theatre*: the sexes were segregated, the women sitting in the upper rows.
62	*Time to Give Up Love* and *But He Can't Face It* are one poem in the MSS.
64	Later Ovid addressed three of his Pontic *Letters* to Graecinus, who was consul in AD 16.
66	*Leda's twins*: Castor and Pollux, protectors of those in danger at sea.
66	*Galatea*: a sea-nymph, daughter of the sea-god Nereus.
70	*duel on the sands of death*: metaphor from gladiatorial combat in the arena. Sand would be spread on the floor to soak up any blood.
70	*Deucalion*: the Greek Noah. He and his wife Pyrrha survived a world flood and repopulated the earth by throwing stones over their shoulders.
70	*Thetis*: Achilles' mother.
70	*Ilia*: mother of Romulus and Remus. See also note on p.98 below.
70	*Caesar . . . Venus*; see note on p.13 above.
72	*witch or . . . wizard*: Circe or Proteus.
78	*Pompeius Macer's* lost epic ended where the *Iliad* begins.
78	*a tragedy*: Ovid's *Medea*, now lost.
78	*the art of love*: most probably the first edition in two books of his *Ars Amatoria*.
78	*love-letters*: there are two collections, *Heroides*, i–xv and xvi–xxi. Nine of the first are mentioned here, including the first Letter and the last.
79	*Laodamia*: wife of Protesilaus whom the gods allowed to visit his wife from the Underworld and she died in the arms of his ghost. See also note on p.57 above.

BOOK THREE

87   *Pelops*: won the hand of Hippodamia by beating her father, the king of Pisa in Elis, in a chariot race. Had the king caught him he would have speared him to death.

87   *The line*: the seats were marked out by grooves in the stone. At the Circus both sexes sat together.

90   *Andromeda*: her mother claimed to be more beautiful than the Nereids, and Neptune punished her by demanding the sacrifice of Andromeda to a sea-monster. She was rescued by Perseus.

91   *Semele*: pregnant with Bacchus she asked her lover Jupiter to appear in all his Olympian glory. Having given his promise Jupiter had to obey, and Semele was burnt to death. But he rescued Bacchus and sewed him up in his thigh till the time came for him to be born.

97   *the hero*: Perseus.

97   *flying wagon*: Ceres gave Triptolemus a chariot drawn by dragons and told him to sow wheat throughout the world.

98   *Ilia*: mother by Mars of Romulus and Remus. Her uncle Amulius ordered the twins to be drowned in the Tiber.

104   *cashed himself*: Jupiter turned himself into a shower of gold to seduce Danae in her tower.

106   In this lament for Tibullus, who died in 19 or 18 BC, each Latin couplet is represented by three short English lines which slow the pace of the poem and add seriousness. In its course there are several allusions to elegies of Tibullus.

109   *Gallus*: the soldier-poet who invented the Latin love elegy. While first Prefect of Egypt he displeased his friend Augustus, was banished and committed suicide in 26 BC. Lycoris was his pseudonym for the dancer Cytheris; see also note on p.41 above.

111   *oracular oak*: the most ancient Greek oracle was the sacred oak of Zeus at Dodona in Epirus.

111   *Cretans*: the Cretan philosopher poet Epimenides (sixth century BC) had written 'Cretans are always liars, evil beasts, slow bellies'.

112   *long-lost daughter*: Proserpina, kidnapped by Pluto on the plain of Enna in Sicily and made his queen in the Underworld. For six months of each year she returned to her mother.

113-14 *Through with Love* and *No, Love Wins* are one poem in the MSS.

123   *Peligni*: they played a leading part in the Social War of 91–87 BC. Their town Corfinium was made the allied capital and renamed Italica. The war compelled the Senate to grant full citizenship to Rome's Italian allies.

123   *high horses*: in this context, announce Ovid's intention to write a tragedy.